The Divine Dance

HOW TO LET GOD LEAD & LEARN HOW TO FOLLOW

Sandra Valenzuela

ZAMIZ PRESS

RELIGION > CHRISTIANITY > DEVOTIONAL

Book Layout © 2017 Book Design Templates
Cover by Alexander Von Ness

Book Layout ©2017 Book Design Templates

The Divine Dance/ Sandra Valenzuela —1st ed.
ISBN 978-1-949813-04-3

Contents

Introduction

This book is a blueprint of sorts, to explore and understand how to have an intimate relationship with God. It's common to hear people say that they have a difficult time hearing God or sensing His will.

Using the analogy of dance, *The Divine Dance* is designed to encourage believers in their quest to keep in step with the Holy Spirit and to enjoy a heightened sensitivity to perceive God's direction and leading in their lives. You have your own unique dance to learn in partnership with our wondrous God. God is inviting you to join Him in the divine dance.

I wait upon the Lord
to hear the beating of His heart.
Like a child being nestled
against her mother's breast
resting in communion with my God.
In that holy place
my ear is opened to His deep
calling out to my deep.
My heart is attuned to God's heartbeat,
and to His voice inviting me
to join Him
in the divine dance.

My Story

When I was 30 years old, I had already walked with the Lord for 14 years. Even though I was growing in my relationship with God, I suffered with a chronic depression that reached back to my childhood. By God's providence, I was connected with a woman who had a deliverance ministry. God used her prayers to bring deliverance to me. I came forth from that deliverance completely set free from depression, suicidal thoughts, and a loss of the will to live. It was like having a dark veil removed from my eyes. Colors were brighter and I was overwhelmed by the beauty of the world around me. I felt the fullness of joy and hope for the first time in my life. I was in awe and wonder of God's delivering power and His amazing love for me. It was the dawn of a new beginning in my life.

I share this pivotal time in my life with you, the reader, to let you know that this is the place from which I write. It is the deep river that began flowing from heaven into me and I will never be the same. This river is for all believers.

It is God's desire and passion to be up close and personal with each one of us. Each of our personal journeys will be different, but God never changes and He is no respecter of persons. This means that

God has an equal and unconditional love for each one of us. God knows just what you need just like He knew what I needed that day. If He did it for me, He will do it for you. Trust Him and look to Him. God will not withhold any good thing from you. My hope for you, dear believer, is that *The Divine Dance* will provide a stepping stone into that new place you've been longing for in your journey with God.

Enjoy the dance,

Sandra Valenzuela

Learning to Listen by Reading God's Word

Let true lovers

break out in praise,

sing out from wherever

they're sitting,

shout the high praises of God,

brandish their swords

in the wild sword-dance--

— Psalm 149:5-6 (The Message)

-DAY 1-

Learning to Listen by Reading God's Word

Suggested reading: Psalm 119:1-16
Scripture focus: Psalm 119:11

Your word I have hidden in my heart, that I might not sin against You. -Psalm 119:11

To know God, the Living Word, you begin by reading His written Word. This is where you will gain understanding and insight into who He really is, not who the world says He is. You should also spend time meditating on God's Word.

To meditate means to speak and repeat God's words. Keep your heart open so God can speak into it. He is eager to speak to you and to show you His ways.

Prayer

Father, open my spiritual senses that I may receive deeper revelation of who You are and what you're saying to me in this hour. How I long to know You in a deeper way. In Jesus' name, amen.

Related scriptures to help you go deeper into God's word:

Joshua 1:8, Psalm 37:31, Psalm 119:23-24

Reflection

Prayerfully ponder: Consider developing a plan to consistently meditate on and memorize scripture.

Thoughts & Prayers

-DAY 2-

Learning to Listen by Reading God's Word

Suggested reading: Isaiah 55:10-11
Scripture focus: Isaiah 55:11

So shall My word be that goes forth
from My mouth;
it shall not return to Me void,
but it shall accomplish what I please,
and it shall prosper in the thing
for which I sent it.
-Isaiah 55:11

There are many treasures hidden in God's word for us, however, it is our responsibility to actively seek and find them. God's word is our road map to the discovery of eternal promises, guidance, hope, healing, and wisdom. As you read, meditate on and speak aloud the word of God. Know that it will go forth and accomplish what God has sent it to do in your life.

Prayer

Father, thank you for Your word of truth that keeps me on the straight and narrow path. Help me to align with Your word in every area of my life.

In Jesus' name, amen.

Related scriptures to help you go deeper into God's word:

Matthew 6:33, Colossians 3:16, Matthew 24:35, Isaiah 49:2, Joshua 21:45

Reflection

Prayerfully ponder: Learn to speak God's word over your current circumstances. Avoid riding the waves of your emotions. Rather, keep your feet planted on God's eternal truth.

Thoughts & Prayers

-DAY 3-

Learning to Listen by Reading God's Word

Suggested reading: Psalm 1
Scripture focus: Psalm 1:2-3

But his delight is in the law of the Lord,
and in His law he meditates day and night.
He shall be like a tree
planted by the rivers of water,
that brings forth its fruit in its season,
whose leaf also shall not wither;
and whatever he does shall prosper. -Psalm 1:2-3

Take hold of God's word. Just as a plant sinks its roots deep into the soil to absorb the nutrients and moisture, sink your roots deep into the truth of His Living Word. Search the Scriptures to understand the intent of God's heart for you.

Prayer

Lord, Your word truly is my delight. It is the food I need to grow and mature in You. Teach me Your ways O' Lord and continue to root me and ground me in Your Living Word.

Related scriptures to help you go deeper into God's word:

Psalm 92:12-14, Jeremiah 17:7-8

Reflection

Prayerfully ponder: What scripture verses from today's devotional can you meditate on? Write them below. What do they mean to you?

Thoughts & Prayers

-DAY 4-

Learning to Listen by Reading God's Word

Suggested reading: Hebrews 4:12-16
Scripture focus: Hebrews 4:12

For the word of God is living and powerful and sharper than any two-edged sword, piercing even to the division of soul and spirit, and of joints and marrow, and is a discerner of the thoughts and intents of the heart. -Hebrews 4:12

The Bible is more than a historical account or a book of rules. It is God's spiritual surgery tool to remove bondages from our lives and bring healing where there was once brokenness. It is His revelatory word to bring light and dispel darkness and deceit. Ask God to open the eyes and the ears of your heart that you may see and hear the truth that will set you free.

Prayer

Lord, please search my heart and show me any areas of darkness. Flood my heart with the light of truth that I may be healed and delivered.

In Jesus' name, amen.

Related scriptures to help you go deeper into God's word:

Psalm 147:15, Ephesians 6:17, Isaiah 50:5, Psalm 107:20

Reflection

Prayerfully ponder: Before reading God's word, ask Him to fill you with the Holy Spirit and give you His eyes to see how it applies to your life.

Thoughts & Prayers

-DAY 5-

Learning to Listen by Reading God's Word

Suggested reading: Deuteronomy 8:2-6
Scripture focus: Deuteronomy 8:3

So He humbled you, allowed you to hunger, and fed you with manna which you did not know nor did your fathers know, that He might make you know that man shall not live by bread alone; but man lives by every word that proceeds from the mouth of the Lord. -Deuteronomy 8:3

The predisposition of human nature is to focus on the external. This also applies to the way we think about our needs. External needs such as food, shelter, clothing, and finances are legitimate, however, if our focus remains on the external alone, it may cause us to overlook the importance of our soul's need for spiritual food. The strength and vitality of the human soul is dependent on the daily nurturance of God's word. Let's not neglect our time with God. Let's feast on His word.

He has much to share with you.

Prayer

Father, please help me to stay in touch with my soul's need for You. Don't let me get lulled to sleep by the desires of my flesh and the cares of this world.

In Jesus' name, amen.

Related scriptures to help you go deeper into God's word:

Matthew 4:4, Exodus 16:2-3,12,14 and
1 Peter 1:24-25

Reflection

Prayerfully ponder: Ask God to show you what internal needs you are masking with external remedies such as overeating, entertainment or shopping. Lay those needs before God and ask Him to bring you healing and restoration.

Thoughts & Prayers

-DAY 6-

Learning to Listen by Reading God's Word

Suggested reading: James 1:22-25
Scripture Verse: James 1:22

But be doers of the word, and not hearers only, deceiving yourselves. - James 1:22

Being a hearer of God's word exclusively is like pouring water into a broken vessel. The Bible's transformative power requires our agreement and participation which includes:

1. Asking God to prepare our hearts to receive what God has for us as we read His word daily.
2. Actively seeking God's wisdom and guidance as we read His word.
3. Aligning our thoughts and actions with God's word by choosing faith over our feelings.
4. Speaking and praying God's word over our daily activities and circumstances.

Prayer

Father, Your word has everything I need. May I be intentional in preparing my heart, aligning my actions, and speaking the truth of your word each day.

In Jesus' name, amen.

Related scriptures to help you go deeper into God's word:

2 Corinthians 3:18, 4:13, 5:7, Romans 8:29, Hebrews 4: 12, Proverbs 18:21

Reflection

Prayerfully ponder: Reflect on how you can use what was shared in today's devotional to more effectively be a doer of the word.

Thoughts & Prayers

-DAY 7-

Learning to Listen by Reading God's Word

Suggested reading: Psalm 119:101-105
Scripture focus: Psalm 119:105

Your word is a lamp to my feet and a light to my path. -Psalm 119:105

Attempting to stay on a path in the dark without a source of light can be a difficult and daunting undertaking at best.

Navigating daily life can be much the same way without the direction and guidance provided by God's written word.

It's easy to believe that you know the best course of action to take in your life, but without feeding on the truth of God's word, it is only a matter of time before you find yourself veering off the path God has set for you. God's word is a spiritual compass for your life journey.

"Trust in the Lord with all your heart,
and lean not on your own understanding; in all your ways acknowledge Him, and He shall direct your paths." -Proverbs 3:5-6

Prayer

Father, I choose to be consistent in studying Your word daily that I may stay on Your path for me.

In Jesus' name, amen.

Related scriptures to help you go deeper into God's word:

Proverbs 3:13, 3:21-26

Reflection

Prayerfully ponder: God's ways are not our ways (Isaiah 55:8-9) and we may not always understand why God is taking us in a certain direction. At that point, we must see the situation through the eyes of faith. What situation do you need to see through faith?

Thoughts & Prayers

Learning to Listen by Seeking God in Prayer

"I'm leaping and singing
in the circle of your love;
you saw my pain, you disarmed my tormenters,
you didn't leave me in their clutches but gave me
room to breathe"
Psalm 31: 7 (The Message)

-DAY 8-

Learning to Listen by Seeking God in Prayer

Suggested reading: Psalm 56
Scripture focus: Psalm 56:9

When I cry out to You, then my enemies will turn back; this I know, because God is for me. - Psalm 56:9

When Jesus was being sought by Judas and the soldiers at the Garden of Gethsemane, He identified himself by saying, "I am He". The soldiers were overcome by the power of Jesus' revelation as God's son and fell to the ground. This same power of the Great I Am (Exodus 3:14) is available to us.

Jesus withholds nothing from His children. All we have to do is ask. As we seek Him with all of our hearts, we can be rest assured that He will fight our battles and turn our enemies back.

If God is for us, who can be against us?

(Romans 8: 31b)

Prayer

Father, thank you for Your love and protection. You are faithful to answer me when I cry out to You. You are so good!

In Jesus' name, amen.

Related scriptures to help you go deeper into God's word:

Hebrews 13:6, Psalm 44:5-7, Psalm 138:7-8, Psalm 84:11

Reflection

Prayerfully ponder: Psalm 118:8 says, "It is better to trust in the Lord than to put confidence in man."

How can you keep your focus on the Lord and put Him first in your life?

Thoughts & Prayers

-DAY 9-

Learning to Listen by Seeking God in Prayer

Suggested reading: Psalm 91:14-16
Scripture focus: Psalm 91:15

He shall call upon Me, and I will answer him,
I will be with him in trouble;
I will deliver him and honor him. -Psalm 91:15

God's promise to us is that when we call upon Him, He will answer us. He promises to be with us whatever we're going through and deliver us. God is faithful to His promises and delights in responding to our prayers. God's deepest desire, however, is to fellowship with us and have an intimate relationship with us.

We need to take inventory and ask ourselves what kind of a relationship we are pursuing with God. Is it a crisis or last resort, a "when we find ourselves in trouble" kind of relationship? Or is it a choice we make daily, to pursue Him and put Him first? Let's put God first in our lives, coming before Him daily in worship and praise with open hearts. Let's choose to love Him and call upon Him each day even when there is no pressing need.

But seek ye first the kingdom of God,
and His righteousness;
and all these things shall be added unto you.
Matthew 6:33 (KJV)

Prayer

Father, please forgive me for the times I have failed to put You first in my life, for the times I've allowed the cares of this world to hold my attention. Please redirect my wayward heart once again.

In Jesus' name, amen.

Related scriptures to help you go deeper into God's word:

Matthew 6:19-21, Luke 10:38-42, 11:9-13

Reflection

Prayerfully ponder: As part of your daily devotions, consider practicing the presence of God by praising and worshiping Him each day. Then spend time in intimate fellowship with Him. This sets the stage for a deeper intimacy with God.

Thoughts & Prayers

-DAY 10-

Learning to Listen by Seeking God in Prayer

Suggested reading and Scripture focus: Psalm 130:1-2

Out of the depths I have cried to You, O Lord;

Lord, hear my voice!

Let Your ears be attentive to the voice of my supplications. - Psalm 130:1-2

What kind of depths are you experiencing in your life right now? Are you in the depths of financial difficulty, the depths of grief due to loss, the depths of health issues, or some tragedy in your life? No matter what we are going through, it is a wonderful truth that our God hears us and is responsive to our cry. In the midst of life's challenges it's important to be aware of the opportunity to go deeper in our relationship with God. He will use our struggles and life issues to bring us to a deeper spiritual maturity and faith.

Let us not forget, even in our darkest moments, that God is good and His plans for us are to prosper and not to harm us (Jeremiah 29:11). May the cry of our hearts be "Lord, take me deeper with You!"

Prayer

Lord, I cry out to You, please take me deeper with You! You are the one I long for. Whatever the cost Lord, have Your way in my life.

In Jesus' name, amen.

Related scriptures to help you go deeper into God's word:

Lamentations 3:55–57, Psalm 143:1

Reflection

Prayerfully ponder: If you're struggling in an area of your life, ask God to show you how He is using it for good.

Thoughts & Prayers

-DAY 11-

Learning to Listen by Seeking God in Prayer

Suggested reading: Ephesians 6:10-18
Scripture focus: Ephesians 6:18

Praying at all times (on every occasion, in every season) in the Spirit, with all [manner of] prayer and entreaty. To that end keep alert and watch with strong purpose and perseverance, interceding in behalf of all the saints (God's consecrated people).
-Ephesians 6:18 (Amplified Bible, Classic Edition)

In this portion of scripture, Paul is speaking passionately about the ministry of prayer. He is speaking as a general rallying and inspiring the troops to prepare for war. Why is Paul's manner of addressing the church so fervent? Paul understood the power of prayer and the importance of adequately preparing to engage in spiritual warfare. The kind of prayer Paul is talking about goes way beyond a quick prayer as you run out the door in the morning. Paul devotes several verses explaining each piece of God's armor and why it is vital to put it on each day, not only for the purpose of prayer but also that we may be able to "successfully stand up against all the strategies and the deceits of the devil." (Ephesians 6:11 Amplified)

We need to come into reality about the fact that Satan wages war against us every day 24/7. We cannot afford to enter our day unprepared. For that reason, we will take time to explore God's armor. Each piece of this armor is God's provision for us through His son, Jesus Christ.

The Helmet of Salvation –

Jesus purchased our salvation when he shed His blood on the cross. God wants our thoughts and plans to be aligned with His. He wants us to have the mind of Christ, (1 Corinthians 2:16). The more we are aligned with God, the more effective our prayers will be.

The Breastplate of Righteousness –

God's righteousness is a gift He gives to us which we receive by faith (Philippians 3:9). We apply this gift of righteousness to our lives by making choices that honor God (1 John 2:29).

The Belt of Truth –

Jesus is the way, the truth, and the life (John 14: 6). The enemy comes to kill, steal, and destroy. He is a liar and the father of lies (John 10:10, John 8:44). This emphasizes the importance of girding ourselves with the truth of God's word. To gird implies preparing for action. Let's be prepared for action by feeding on God's word daily.

The Gospel of Peace –

The gospel is the good news of Jesus paying for the penalty of our sins and providing us with peace that is not of this world (John 14: 27). As we embrace the hope of the gospel and walk in God's peace, we can then effectively and with intention, bring hope and peace to this fallen world.

The Shield of Faith –

God has given us free will to choose to believe in Him. It is through faith that we quench the fiery darts of the enemy. Faith is the key to overcoming and having victory in our lives (1 John 5: 4).

The Sword of the Spirit (the Word of God, Hebrews 4:12) –

The Bible is God's love letter to us. He has given it to us to provide instruction and guidance for our daily lives. In order for us to pray effectively, we must prepare ourselves by putting on the full armor of God.

Prayer

Father, help me to be consistent in prayer and in putting on the spiritual armor daily.

In Jesus' name, amen.

Related scriptures to help you go deeper into God's word:

2 Corinthians 6:7, Isaiah 11:5, 1 Peter 1:13, Romans 13:12, Isaiah 59:17

Reflection

Prayerfully ponder: How can you make it a habit to put God's armor on daily?

Thoughts & Prayers

-DAY 12-

Learning to Listen by Seeking God in Prayer

Suggested reading and Scripture focus: Psalm 5:1-3

Give ear to my words, O Lord,
consider my meditation.
Give heed to the voice of my cry,
my King and my God.
For to You I will pray.
My voice You shall hear in the morning,
O Lord; in the morning I will direct it to You, and I will look up. -Psalm 5:1-3

David's prayer says a lot about his relationship with the Lord. He is crying out to God asking Him to hear not only his prayer but also the intention of his heart. He refers to God as his King which shows his willingness to submit to and serve Him. David uses the word "direct" referring to his intention to focus his prayers towards God each morning. Direct is the Hebrew word "arak" which refers to placing things in order or to an army preparing for battle. These definitions suggest that David was praying with intention and had a daily prayer strategy.

The final line in verse 3 says, "And I will look up" which indicates that David was waiting for and anticipating an answer to his prayer. He was a man of faith and approached God with an expectant heart.

Prayer

Lord, I come with a heart full of intention to connect with You. I wait with anticipation and expectation to hear Your heart and to know Your will.

Related scriptures to help you go deeper into God's word:

Psalm 4:1, Job 42:10, Romans 12:12

Reflection

Prayerfully ponder: God wants us to come "boldly to the throne of grace that we may obtain mercy and find grace to help in time of need" (Hebrews 4: 16). God is always ready to have fellowship with us and He is eager to hear and respond to our prayers. What do you need from God today?

Thoughts & Prayers

-DAY 13-

Learning to Listen by Seeking God in Prayer

Suggested reading: 2 Chronicles 7:1-15
Scripture focus: 2 Chronicles 7:14

If My people who are called by My name will humble themselves, and pray and seek My face, and turn from their wicked ways, then I will hear from heaven, and will forgive their sin and heal their land.

-2 Chronicles 7:14

In this passage God is speaking to Solomon in response to his prayer of dedication of the temple. God appears to Solomon and gives him specific instructions on how the people are to pray in order for Israel to receive God's blessing.

This conditional promise began with the requirement that God's people humble themselves which in this context means to make low. This refers to a person who is willingly submitted to God and His will.

The second requirement is that the people pray. The Hebrew word, *palal,* describes prayer as intercession, asking someone with more power and wisdom to intervene.

The third requirement is to seek God's face. What does it mean to seek God's face? To seek means to search for, try to find, look for, be after, to go in quest of. With our closest loved ones and friends, we can usually take one look at them and discern how they're feeling or when they're troubled. We know them well. We've spent many hours, over many years, getting to know them intimately. This is the cry of God's heart that we, as His people, would come to know Him that way. Seeking God's face is motivated by our yearning for intimate knowledge of God. God wants to be known by us.

Finally, they were to turn from their "wicked ways". God required the people to repent of their sins and turn back to Him.

God is eager to answer our prayers and we are abundantly blessed because Jesus paid the penalty for our sins. Let's humble ourselves before God, seek His face, and turn away from those things that are displeasing to Him. Let's position ourselves to receive all that God has for us.

Prayer

Father, it is an amazing truth that You desire an intimate relationship with me. Lord, I say yes!

In Jesus' name, amen.

Related scriptures to help you go deeper into God's word:

1 Samuel 1:12, Isaiah 38:2-3, Jonah 2:1-9

Reflection

Prayerfully ponder: To help you remember 2 Chronicles 7:14, you may want to think of this verse as a recipe for blessing:

- Humility
- Prayer
- Seek
- Repent

Thoughts & Prayers

-DAY 14-

Learning to Listen by Seeking God in Prayer

Suggested reading: Philippians 4:4-9
Scripture focus: Philippians 4:6-7

Be anxious for nothing, but in everything by prayer and supplication, with thanksgiving, let your requests be made known to God; and the peace of God, which surpasses all understanding, will guard your hearts and minds through Christ Jesus.

-Philippians 4:6-7

God does not want us to dwell on the things that we are tempted to become anxious about. He wants us to turn our worries into prayer. We may feel the need to cry out before Him as we lay our requests at His feet. 1 Peter 5:7 says, "Cast all your cares upon Him, for He cares for you." To cast means to "throw off" in this context. Let's learn to throw off our cares and concerns and leave them before God. Go before God in prayer. Ask Him to take your burden and then exercise your faith by trusting God to take care of it. We can then be free to thank God for the answers He will bring and for His faithfulness in all things. God promises to then give us peace and protect our hearts and minds.

Prayer

Lord, I choose to cast all my cares on You and entrust all the issues of my life to You. Have your way O Lord, have Your way.

In Jesus' name, amen.

Related scriptures to help you go deeper into God's word:

Matthew 6:25, 1 Thessalonians 5:17, 18, John 14:27

Reflection

Prayerfully ponder: Read Isaiah 26:3-4 for more biblical guidance on walking in God's peace.

Thoughts & Prayers

Learning to Listen by Waiting on God

I've kept my feet on the ground,

I've cultivated a quiet heart,

Like a baby content in its mother's arms,

my soul is a baby content.

-Psalm 131:2 (The Message)

-DAY 15-

Learning to Listen by Waiting on God

Suggested reading: Psalm 27
Scripture focus: Psalm 27:14

Wait on the Lord;
be of good courage,
and He shall strengthen your heart;
wait I say on the Lord!
-Psalm 27:14

To wait on the Lord means to wait in faith. You must have faith in God's character, faith in His word, and faith in His promises. Seeing the situation through the eyes of faith means to align your heart and mind with God's perspective. To be of "good courage" in the context of this verse means to be strong and not faint or be dismayed. As we wait on God, He is faithful to provide all the strength we need.

"But those who wait on the Lord
shall renew their strength;
they shall mount up with wings like eagles,
they shall run and not be weary,
they shall walk and not faint."
-Isaiah 40:31

Prayer

Father, please forgive me for the many times I have allowed impatience to overcome me when I should have waited on you. I need your help to wait with faith and patience.

In Jesus' name, amen.

Related scriptures to help you go deeper into God's word:

Psalm 25:3, Proverbs 20:22, Psalm 62:5

Reflection

Prayerfully ponder: Do you realize that hearing and discerning God's voice is not the gift of a few, but a learned discipline of patiently waiting and listening to God? Consider taking a few minutes today to wait and listen.

Thoughts & Prayers

-DAY 16-

Learning to Listen by Waiting on God

Suggested reading: Psalm 130
Scripture focus: Psalm 130:5-6

I wait for the Lord, my soul waits,

and in His word I do hope.

My soul waits for the Lord

more than those who watch for the morning-

yes, more than those who watch for the morning.

-Psalm 130:5-6

The impassioned plea of the psalmist is for God to respond to his cry as he waits with expectation and hope. There is a sense of desperation and intense longing in the psalmist's expression, "More than those who watch for the morning, yes, more than those who watch for the morning". The psalmist is referring to night watchmen standing guard over the city, waiting anxiously for the break of day so they can be relieved of watch duty.

When we have waited patiently in the valley of suffering or sorrow, we can identify with the longing for a glimpse of hope and comfort. A light at the end of the tunnel. It is reassuring to know that even in those times, God is our refuge and strength, a very present help in trouble (Psalm 46:1). He is Immanuel, God with us (Matthew 1:23) and He promises to never leave us nor forsake us (Hebrews 13:5).

Prayer

Thank you, Lord, that even in the dark night of the soul we can rejoice and take comfort in the truth of Your word.

Related scriptures to help you go deeper into God's word:

Lamentations 3:26

Reflection

Prayerfully ponder: Psalm 23 is a good psalm to meditate on during difficult times.

Thoughts & Prayers

-DAY 17-

Learning to Listen by Waiting on God

Suggested reading: Isaiah 30:18-21
Scripture focus: Isaiah 30:18

Therefore the Lord will wait,
that He may be gracious to you;
And therefore He will be exalted,
that He may have mercy on you.
For the Lord is a God of justice;
blessed are all those who wait for Him.
-Isaiah 30:18

Judah's leaders were relying on their alliance with Egypt to protect them from Assyria instead of relying on God. Even in their misguided behavior God waited to be gracious to the Israelites.

We often think in terms of how challenging it can be to wait on God's timing in our lives. How often do we consider the reality that God waits for us, to be gracious and merciful to us even in times of willful sin and rebellion? Our God continues to reach out to humankind with His everlasting love, though many reject Him and turn to other gods.

God waits, His arms ready to embrace and restore us. So, the next time we are tempted to get discouraged while waiting for God's intervention, we must remember He has also waited for us and He is always faithful.

Prayer

Father, your all-encompassing love for me is amazing! That You wait for us to come to You so You can show us mercy and grace is a beautiful picture of the depth of Your love for us. Thank you, Lord!

In Jesus' name, amen.

Related scriptures to help you go deeper into God's word:
Isaiah 33:2, Proverbs 3:5-6, Jeremiah 9:23-24

Reflection

Prayerfully ponder: While waiting on God, how can you focus on how He has blessed you and express gratitude?

Thoughts & Prayers

-DAY 18-

Learning to Listen by Waiting on God

Suggested reading: Psalm 37
Scripture focus: Psalm 37:7

Rest in the Lord, and wait patiently for Him;
Do not fret because of him who prospers in his way,
because of the man who brings
wicked schemes to pass.
-Psalm 37:7

As we rest in the truth of God's word, believing in His promises to us, we can truly be at peace. Keeping our focus on Jesus, our anchor in the storm of life's pressures and problems, let us Be still and know that He is God (Psalm 46:10). When we are tempted to take matters into our own hands it would be in our best interest to remember that God is always faithful to intervene in His perfect timing.

"Let us hold fast the confession of our hope
without wavering,
for He who promised is faithful."
-Hebrews 10:23

Prayer

Yes, Lord, You are always faithful. I choose to keep my focus on You in my current circumstances. I will hope in You and fix my heart on your promises.

In Jesus' name, amen.

Related scriptures to help you go deeper into God's word:

Psalm 25:21, Psalm 37:34, Proverbs 3:5-6

Reflection

Prayerfully ponder: What does it mean to rest in the Lord?

Thoughts & Prayers

-DAY 19-

Learning to Listen by Waiting on God

Suggested reading: Micah 7
Scripture focus: Micah 7:7

But as for me, I will look to the Lord
and confident in Him I will keep watch; I will wait
with hope and expectancy for
the God of my salvation; my God will hear me.
-Micah 7:7 (Amplified Bible, Classic Edition)

Having confidence in God keeps us from worrying and is a reinforcement to our faith. Confidence also builds our strength as we wait on God. Hope and expectancy are the fruit of our confidence in God and we can be assured that He hears the prayer of the righteous (Proverbs 15: 29.) Be encouraged as you wait on God, knowing He keeps His promises and His word is true.

Prayer

Father, it's easy for me to place my confidence in what I can see, but I know these things are temporary and fleeting. Your love is everlasting, faithful and unchanging. Help me to always choose You, Lord.

In Jesus' name, amen.

Related scriptures to help you go deeper into God's word:

Isaiah 30:15, Hebrews 4:16, 13:5, Isaiah 26:3

Reflection

Prayerfully ponder: In Isaiah 30:15 it says, "In returning and rest you shall be saved; In quietness and confidence shall be your strength." How can you apply this truth to your current life circumstance?

Thoughts & Prayers

A Teachable Heart

"David, ceremonially dressed in
priest's linen, danced
with great abandon
before God".
-2 Samuel 6:12-16 (The Message)

-DAY 20-

A Teachable Heart

Suggested reading: Psalm 25:8-11
Scripture focus: Psalm 25:8-9

Good and upright is the Lord;

Therefore He teaches sinners in the way.

The humble He guides in justice,

and the humble He teaches His way.

-Psalm 25:8-9

The attribute of being humble is vital to growing in the Lord. To be humble means to be meek and submissive rather than proud or arrogant. When we approach God in this way we are open to receive His direction and counsel. We become pliable in His hands, so that God is able to bend and mold us into His image. "But now, O Lord, You are our Father; we are the clay, and You our potter; and all we are the work of Your hand." Isaiah 64:8

In Matthew 18:3 Jesus says, "...unless you are converted and become as little children, you will by no means enter the kingdom of heaven. Therefore, whoever humbles himself as this little child is the greatest in the kingdom of heaven." The innocence of children and their simple trust, is the way in which we need to posture ourselves in God's presence. That is a picture of a teachable heart.

Prayer

Father, please restore a simple, childlike faith in me, that I may be easily led by You. Restore innocence to my heart that I would be humble and teachable.

In Jesus' name, amen.

Related scriptures to help you go deeper into God's word:

Psalm 147:6, James 4:6 & 10, Peter 5:5-6

Reflection

Prayerfully ponder: Read Isaiah 57:15. What does this verse say to you about being humble?

Thoughts & Prayers

-DAY 21-

A Teachable Heart

Suggested reading: Proverbs 3:1-8
Scripture focus: Proverbs 3:7-8

Do not be wise in your own eyes;

fear the Lord and depart from evil.

It will be health to your flesh,

And strength to your bones. -Proverbs 3:7-8

Why shouldn't we think of ourselves as wise and be self-confident in our own abilities? Isn't it God who has given us our giftings to do great things for Him? The fear of the Lord as used in this verse refers to discipline or the instruction of wisdom. The fear of the Lord means to have an absolute and profound respect for almighty God.

As we posture ourselves in this way before God, we must come to the conclusion that He is sovereign over our lives and we dare not go forward in any endeavor without submitting all of ourselves to Him.

It is important to consider Isaiah 55:8-9, "For My thoughts are not your thoughts, nor are your ways My ways," says the Lord. "For as the heavens are higher than the earth, so are My ways higher than your ways, and My thoughts than your thoughts."

The truth is that God has given us giftings and abilities to use for His glory, but in great humility we lay it all before Him, trusting that He knows best how to navigate our lives.

Prayer

Not my way, but Your way O Lord. Not for me but for You alone, for You alone.

In Jesus' name, amen.

Related scriptures to help you go deeper into God's word:
Proverbs 15:33, Proverbs 16:18-19, Proverbs 19:23

Reflection

Prayerfully ponder: Consider finding a daily quiet time with God, to pray and listen.

Thoughts & Prayers

-DAY 22-

A Teachable Heart

Suggested reading: Proverbs 19:20-23
Scripture focus: Proverbs 19:20

Hear counsel, receive instruction and accept correction, that you may be wise in the time to come.
-Proverbs 19:20 (Amplified Bible, Classic Edition)

A teachable heart is bendable and pliable. We must bend to God's will even though we may not understand. We can depend on the fact that there will be times when our flesh will want to do the exact opposite of what God is saying. It's not always easy to align our natural instincts with God's divine nature. For that reason, God sent His Holy Spirit to abide in us.

Jesus described the Holy Spirit as our helper. Inherent in the Greek word for helper (parakletos) is the Holy Spirit as our advocate, comforter, protector, teacher, counselor, and guide. As we submit to Holy Spirit's influence within us, we will be progressively transformed into God's image.

Prayer

Father, give me a tender and submissive heart towards You. May my heart be pliable in Your hands.

In Jesus' name, amen.

Related scriptures to help you go deeper into God's word:
Psalm 32:37, Psalm 37:37, Proverbs 11:14

Reflection

Prayerfully ponder: Ask God to show you any heart issues that may be hindering your ability to hear and receive God's counsel and instruction.

Thoughts & Prayers

-DAY 23-

A Teachable Heart

Suggested reading: Psalm 86
Scripture focus: Psalm 86:11

Teach me Your way, O Lord; that I may walk and live in Your truth; direct and unite my heart [solely, reverently] to fear and honor Your name.
-Psalm 86:11 (Amplified Bible, Classic Edition)

Learning to walk in God's ways begins with a heart of humility, determination, and obedience. David demonstrates this quality of humility as he cries out to God with an open heart to be taught in His ways. David declares with a heart of determination that he will walk in God's truth. Finally, David asks that his heart be united (with a singleness of heart) to deeply reverence (have respect for) God. This is a heart of obedience.

Prayer

Father, break down every wall in my heart that resists humility and obedience to You. Teach me Your ways, God, for I am determined to be completely Yours.

In Jesus' name, amen.

Related scriptures to help you go deeper into God's word:

Psalm 27:11, Psalm 143:8

Reflection

Prayerfully ponder: Ask the Lord to make your heart completely His and to show you any barriers that may be hindering this process.

Thoughts & Prayers

Letting God Lead

Teach me to dance, Lord

Show me your way,

In the night seasons

Or the dawn of the day.

Stretch me or bend me

I submit to Your lead

Do what You want to

I long to be freed.

-DAY 24-

Letting God Lead

Suggested reading: Psalm 23
Scripture focus: Psalm 23:1-2

The Lord is my shepherd;
I shall not want.
He makes me to lie down in green pastures;
He leads me beside the still waters. -Psalm 23:1-2

The role of a shepherd is to lead, protect, and provide for the sheep. David says in verse 1 that he shall not want (lack anything) as he follows the Lord his shepherd. Jesus identified Himself as the good shepherd who lays His life down for the sheep (John 10:11). Even in the midst of life's trials and pressures, Jesus our good shepherd, desires to lead us to places of rest and refreshment (Psalm 23:2). He desires to give us an abundant life so we would not lack any good thing (John 10:10).

What's key in the above verses is our response to God's desire to be our good shepherd. Consider the following questions:

1. Are you willing to let God lead you?
2. Do you trust Him to do what's best for you?
3. Are you taking time to hear what God is saying to you each day? (John 10:4)

If we find ourselves stressed out and exhausted, it's time to take a step back. It's time to "Be still and know that I am God" (Psalm 46:10). God is always ready to bring peace and refreshment to us. He is ready to bring order into our lives. He's ready to protect and provide for us. The question is, are we ready to let Him?

"My sheep hear My voice and I know them,
and they follow Me." -John 10:27

Prayer

Father, forgive me for trying to control my circumstances and figure everything out. Please help me to let go and let you lead the way.

In Jesus' name, amen.

Related scriptures to help you go deeper into God's word:

Psalm 65:11-13, Psalm 78:52-53, Philippians 4:19, Revelation 7:17

Reflection

Prayerfully ponder: Spend time resting with Jesus today. Pour out your heart before Him and receive all He has for you.

Thoughts & Prayers

-DAY 25-

Letting God Lead

Suggested reading: Romans 8:12-17
Scripture focus: Romans 8:14

For as many as are led by the Spirit of God, these are sons of God. -Romans 8:14

Paul is exhorting believers to put to death the deeds of the flesh in order to walk in the Spirit and live. In this context being led by the Spirit of God implies progressively putting to death the fleshly appetites of the lower nature. As we do so, we are making room in ourselves for the Holy Spirit to increasingly lead us. The increasing influence of Holy Spirit within us empowers us to conform to God's ways. It's the difference between only having an external objective knowledge of God's word and working hard to meets God's standards, and having the extra benefit of an internal sensitivity to the leading of the Holy Spirit in our daily lives.

Prayer

Father, take me to a deeper place with You. Cause me to have a deeper sensitivity to the leading of Your Holy Spirit. I need more of You and less of me Lord, for Your glory.

In Jesus' name, amen.

Related scriptures to help you go deeper into God's word:

Galatians 5:16-25

Reflection

Prayerfully ponder: What does, "more of You, less of me" mean in your daily walk with God?

Thoughts & Prayers

-DAY 26-

Letting God Lead

Suggested reading: Psalm 25
Scripture focus: Psalm 25:5

Lead me in Your truth and teach me,
for You are the God of my salvation;
on You I wait all the day. -Psalm 25:5

With an open and submissive heart David asks God to lead and teach him His truth. It requires humility to ask to be led.

Inherent in this request is a letting go of one's own ways and independent will, in favor of the Master's.

David addresses God as "the God of my salvation." The word salvation in this verse refers to immediate deliverance from adversity. David demonstrates a deep trust in God's ability and faithfulness to deliver him from his enemies and makes a declaration that he waits on God all day long. The word wait, in this context, is to wait with expectation. By faith, David is fully expecting God to come through for him.

Prayer

Father, I echo David's cry, please lead me and teach me to walk in Your ways. I gladly lay down my ways and submit to Your direction in my life. Increase my faith, Lord, to trust You in all things.

In Jesus' name, amen.

Related scriptures to help you go deeper into God's word:

Psalm 32:8, Psalm 34:6, Psalm 9:10

Reflection

Prayerfully ponder: How did God speak to you through today's devotional?

Thoughts & Prayers

Learning the Steps

You did it: you changed wild lament
into whirling dance;
you ripped off my black mourning band
and decked me with wildflowers.
I'm about to burst with song;
I can't keep quiet about you.
God, my God, I can't thank you enough.
-Psalm 30:11-12 (The Message)

-DAY 27-

Learning the Steps

Suggested reading: Psalm 37:23-29
Scripture focus: Psalm 37:23-24

The steps of a good man are ordered by the Lord,
and He delights in his way.
Though he fall, he shall not be utterly cast down;
for the Lord upholds him with His hand.
-Psalm 37:23-24

God directs the steps of those who walk in His ways, who seek first His kingdom and trust in Him. God delights in those who are completely His. Though even the righteous may stumble and fall, God is faithful to hold up and watch over His beloved ones. God is faithful to finish what He has started in our lives. (Philippians 1:6)

Prayer

Lord, thank you for Your faithfulness and goodness to me. I trust You to order my steps so I can fulfill all that You have called me to for Your glory.

Related scriptures to help you go deeper into God's word:

Psalm 40:2, Psalm 91:11-12, Proverbs 3:5-6, Matthew 6:33, Acts 5:29

Reflection

Prayerfully ponder: "The fear of the Lord is the beginning of wisdom, and the knowledge of the Holy One is understanding." Proverbs 9:10.

Thoughts & Prayers

-DAY 28-

Learning the Steps

Suggested reading: 1 Peter 2:11-25
Scripture focus: 1 Peter 2:21-24

For to this you were called, because Christ also suffered for us, leaving us an example, that you should follow His steps:
"Who committed no sin,
nor was deceit found in His mouth,"

who, when He was reviled, did not revile in return; when He suffered, He did not threaten, but committed Himself to Him who judges righteously, who Himself bore our sins in His own body on the tree, that we, having died to sins, might live for righteousness – by whose stripes you were healed. -1 Peter 2:21-24

Sometimes walking in the steps of Jesus may bring us into difficult places. When we experience difficulties, our flesh is more likely to cause us to lash out at others. Peter offers instruction and guidance to us as demonstrated by the character of Jesus during His time of suffering:

1. Jesus did not commit sins.
2. No deceit was found in His mouth.
3. Jesus did not verbally attack (revile) those who reviled Him.
4. He did not threaten His accusers.

It is only by our submission to the Holy Spirit of God that we are able to walk in Jesus' steps. James 4:6b-7 says, "God resists the proud, but gives grace to the humble. Therefore submit to God. Resist the devil and he will flee from you." As we humble ourselves before God and submit to His leading in our lives, God gives us strength to turn away from the influence of Satan's temptation.

Prayer

Father, I want Your ways to be my ways. My desire is to align with You in every area of my life. Help me to choose You each day.

In Jesus' name, amen.

Related scriptures to help you go deeper into God's word:

Proverbs 3:34, 1 Peter 5:5-6, James 4:6-7

Reflection

Prayerfully ponder: Write down some experiences you've had walking through difficult situations and how God helped you through the journey.

Thoughts & Prayers

-DAY 29-

Learning the Steps

Suggested reading: Proverbs 16:1-9
Scripture focus: Proverbs 16:9

A man's heart plans his way,

but the Lord directs his steps.

-Proverbs 16:9

As we plot our life's journey, making plans and setting future goals, it is imperative to lay them at God's feet. As we submit them before the Lord, may we open our hearts in humility and say, "Let your will be done O' Lord." Then in obedience, let us listen and respond to the Master's voice.

Prayer

Lord, I only want to walk in Your steps and listen for Your voice to guide me along life's path. For me, there is no other way but Your way.

In Jesus' name, amen.

Related scriptures to help you go deeper into God's word:

Psalm 16:20, Psalm 17:5, Proverbs 20:24,
Jeremiah 10:23-24

Reflection

Prayerfully ponder: What is God's next step for you?

Thoughts & Prayers

A
New Song

Praise the Lord!
Sing to the Lord a new song,
and His praise in the
assembly of saints
-Psalm 149:1

-DAY 30-

A New Song

Suggested reading: Psalm 98
Scripture focus: Psalm 98:1

Oh, sing to the Lord a new song!
For He has done marvelous things;
His right hand and His holy arm
have gained Him the victory. -Psalm 98:1

A new song is born out of the overflow of our praise and worship, when God gives us a new way of thanking Him in song. As demonstrated in the previous verse, a new song was often sung during a time of victory. There are also times when God will require us to break out in a new song of victory before the breakthrough comes.

That is a powerful weapon and an act of faith. What song of victory is God calling you to sing today? As you sing your victory song, know that God is fighting for you and the victory is already yours through faith in our Lord Jesus Christ.

"For all the promises of God in Him are Yes, and in Him Amen, to the glory of God through us."

-2 Corinthians 1:20

Prayer

Father, thank you for the new songs you provide so that we can go deeper in worship and ultimately break through to victory.

In Jesus Name, amen.

Related scriptures to help you go deeper into God's word:
Psalm 33:1-3, Isaiah 42:10-13

Reflection

Prayerfully ponder: What is your current battlefield? Sing a song of victory over it. Consider writing down your victory song below.

Thoughts & Prayers

-DAY 31-

A New Song

Suggested reading: 2 Samuel 6
Scripture focus: 2 Samuel 6:14-15

Then David danced before the Lord with all his might, and David was wearing a linen ephod. So David and all the house of Israel brought up the ark of the Lord with shouting and with the sound of the trumpet. -2 Samuel 6:14-15

David did a spontaneous dance before God to celebrate the ark of God being brought back to the temple. He wore only a linen ephod and danced with "all his might". David did not follow the dictates of tradition as it was normally women who danced when the occasion called for it. It was unheard of for a king to dance in such a manner in public. It was clear that David's sole concern was to worship the Lord through dance regardless of people's opinions. There are times when God will call us out of our comfort zones, to do something for Him.

God has made each one of us unique. He did not create us to be carbon copies of one another. What is God calling you to do? I sense in my heart that God is calling some of you to a new place and has given you dreams that you've been hesitant to pursue, after all, no one else is doing that unique thing. You wonder, what if I'm wrong?

Let me encourage you to dare to believe and trust God to bring you step-by-step into the unique thing He's calling you to. Be diligent to pray over your dreams and desires. If it's God's will, He will bring it to pass.

Prayer

Father, please bring me into the new thing you have for me. I lay it at Your feet and I trust You to guide me each step of the way.

In Jesus Name, amen.

Related scriptures to help you go deeper into God's word:

Exodus 15:1-21

Reflection

Prayerfully ponder: What is God calling you to do? Write down some future dreams you believe God has given to you. Spend some time praying over them.

Thoughts & Prayers

A Final Word

I hope you enjoyed your journey through *The Divine Dance.* Each daily devotion could easily be extended into 2 sessions. If you didn't do that the first time, I encourage you to read through *The Divine Dance* again, taking more time to meditate on each scripture. Also, take time to consider the information provided in each "prayerfully ponder" section and journal your prayers and thoughts to God. Take time to listen to God's responses to your prayers and write them down. May your joy be full and your hearts be merry as you join God in the divine dance.

Many blessings,

Sandra Valenzuela

Have you enjoyed this devotional? Check out Sandra's debut devotional *Romancing the Divine,* available wherever books are sold or at https://amzn.to/2TlfBKV.

ABOUT THE AUTHOR

Sandra Valenzuela is a licensed clinical social worker who has been in the mental health field for over 25 years. She has a private practice in Kingsburg, California. She has been providing biblically-based Christian counseling for the past 16 years. Sandra lives in Reedley, California, with Michael, her husband of 40 years.

You can connect with Sandra through email at sandrav56@yahoo.com.

CPSIA information can be obtained
at www.ICGtesting.com
Printed in the USA
FSHW011223100519
58021FS